IT'S COOL TO LEARN ABOUT COUNTRIES

Social Studies Explorer

INDONESIA

◆ by Tamra Orr

CHERRY LAKE PUBLISHING • ANN ARBOR, MICHIGAN

Published in the United States of America
by Cherry Lake Publishing
Ann Arbor, Michigan
www.cherrylakepublishing.com

Content Adviser: Rudolf Mrázek, PhD, Associate Professor,
Department of Southeast Asian Studies, University of Wisconsin-Madison

Book design: The Design Lab

Photo credits: Cover, top, ©iStockphoto.com/btrenkel; Cover, bottom, back cover, pages 3,
5, 10, 16, 20, 24, 34, 35 and 48, ©iStockphoto.com/raclro; page 4, ©jfperon/Shutterstock,
Inc.; page 7, ©iStockphoto.com/helovi; page 8, ©Hywit Dimyadi/Shutterstock, Inc; page 9,
©Art Directors & TRIP/Alamy; page 11, ©kkaplin/Shutterstock, Inc.; page 14, ©Andrey
Ushakov/Shutterstock, Inc.; page 15, ©iStockphoto.com/technotr; page 16, ©iStockphoto/
antoniodalbore; page 17, ©Mike Abrahams/Alamy; page 19, ©Friday/Dreamstime.com; page
21, ©AK Photo/Shutterstock, Inc.; page 23, ©RIA Novosti/Alamy; page 25, ©iStockphoto.com/
DistinctiveImages; page 26, ©iStockphoto.com/BartCo; page 27, ©Images & Stories/Alamy;
page 29, ©Yuliang/Dreamstime.com; page 30, ©Distinctive Images/Shutterstock, Inc.; page
31, ©ayazad/Shutterstock, Inc.; page 32, ©Peter Horree/Alamy; page 33, ©Andreyushakov/
Dreamstime.com; page 38, ©Peter Treanor/Alamy; pages 40 and 42, ©Teng Wei/Shutterstock,
Inc.; page 41, ©Ly Dinh Quoc Vu/Shutterstock, Inc.; page 44, ©Bare Essence Photography/
Alamy; page 45, ©Gabriel Nardelli Araujo/Shutterstock, Inc.

Library of Congress Cataloging-in-Publication Data
Orr, Tamra.
  It's cool to learn about countries—Indonesia/by Tamra Orr.
     p. cm.—(Social studies explorer)
  Includes index.
  ISBN-13: 978-1-60279-826-7 (lib. bdg.)
  ISBN-10: 1-60279-826-5 (lib. bdg.)
1. Indonesia—Juvenile literature. I. Title. II. Title: Indonesia. III. Series.
  DS615.078 2010
  959.8—dc22   2009048067

Cherry Lake Publishing would like to acknowledge the work of The Partnership for 21st
Century Skills. Please visit www.21stcenturyskills.org for more information.

Printed in the United States of America
Corporate Graphics Inc.
July 2010
CLFA07

TABLE OF CONTENTS

CHAPTER ONE

WELCOME TO INDONESIA!

➤ There are thousands of islands to explore in Indonesia!

Have you ever thought about going to Indonesia? If you go, you should pack a swimsuit. That's because Indonesia is not one large land mass. Instead, it is made up of nearly 18,000 islands scattered across thousands of miles of oceans and seas. Only about one-third of the islands, however, have people living on them.

If you went to Indonesia, you could stop by the three lakes of Kelimutu to see the ever-changing colors of their waters. You could also stop to see a shadow puppet show. Are you hungry? Grab a snack from one of the street vendors calling out for your attention. If you go during the wet season, take an umbrella. Bring shorts during the dry season—it is hot and humid. Let's explore Indonesia!

Many islands make up the **archipelago** of Indonesia. If you visited a different island each day, it would take nearly 50 years to see each one!

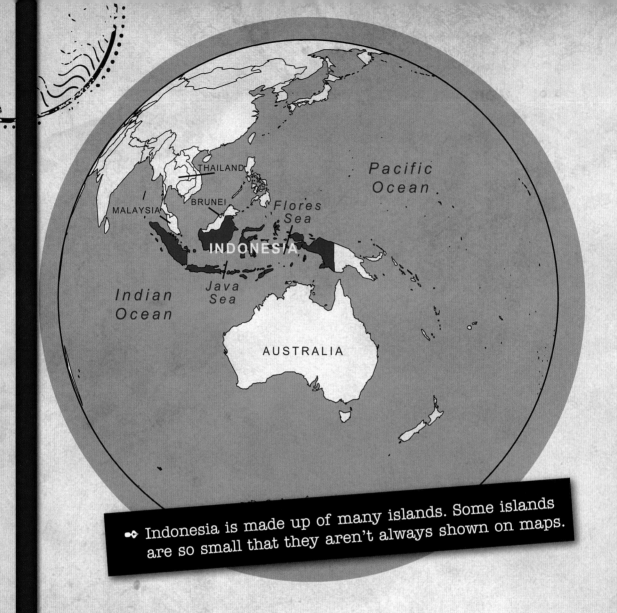

THAILAND

BRUNEI

MALAYSIA

Flores
Sea

Pacific
Ocean

INDONESIA

Indian
Ocean

Java
Sea

AUSTRALIA

➴ Indonesia is made up of many islands. Some islands are so small that they aren't always shown on maps.

Pointing to Indonesia on a globe is tricky. Its islands stretch out like a string of emeralds across the Indian and Pacific Oceans, as well as the Java and Flores Seas. Nearby countries include Thailand, Malaysia, Brunei, and Australia. Indonesia covers approximately 735,358 square miles (1,904,569 square kilometers). That is nearly three times the size of Texas.

Two-thirds of Indonesia's islands have nothing on them other than plants and animals. Despite this, Indonesia has a population of more than 240 million. Most people live on the Greater and Lesser Sunda Islands. These include Sumatra, Java, Kalimantan, and Sulawesi.

�~ Many people on the island of Sumatra still live in traditional villages.

Java is the most modern island. It is about the same size as the state of New York. Jakarta, the country's capital and largest city, is found here. In many ways, Jakarta looks just like any large city with skyscrapers and traffic problems.

Sumatra is the sixth largest island in the world. It is a land of striking differences. You'll find rice fields that color the landscape with shifting shades of green. There are also stark volcanic craters. In recent years, this part of Indonesia has been hit hard by earthquake damage.

Oceans are not the only bodies of water that affect Indonesia. The islands also have amazing rivers and lakes. Some of these waterways are used for transportation. People travel across them using motorized canoes and bamboo rafts. The waters of the three Kelimutu lakes are especially fascinating. Although they are located next to each other, they are completely different colors. Without warning, the waters shift colors. Why? One theory is that when minerals in the water dissolve and the acidity changes, the colors change. Possible shades include turquoise, burgundy, and dark blue.

Kelimutu's colorful lakes offer a breathtaking view to the many tourists who visit the volcano.

As wonderful as the oceans around Indonesia's islands are, they can also be dangerous. In 2004, a tidal wave was created by a 9.0 magnitude earthquake under the Indian Ocean. It moved across the water at the speed of a jet plane. More than 150,000 people were killed or missing by the end of the day. It was the most destructive **tsunami** in recorded history.

There was once a volcanic island named Krakatoa between Java and Sumatra. From May to August 1883, the island rumbled with earthquakes. Then the volcano exploded four times, destroying the entire island. The blast was equal to a 100-megaton nuclear bomb. More than 165 villages on nearby islands were destroyed. Much of the damage was caused by the 115-foot (35 meter) tidal wave that followed.

•• Rafflesia may look beautiful, but beware of its terrible smell!

One reason Indonesia is so lovely is that it is home to more than 40,000 species of flowering plants. One very special flower is the rafflesia. It is the largest flower in the world. It grows to be more than 3 feet (0.9 m) wide and can weigh as much as 20 pounds (9.1 kilograms). Its claim to fame, however, is its smell. Are you thinking of a pleasant fragrance? Think again! In order to attract insects and be pollinated, the flower puts out an odor similar to that of rotting meat. No wonder its nickname is the **corpse** flower!

ACTIVITY

THAILAND

MALAYSIA

South China Sea

BRUNEI

MALAYSIA

Aceh

Sumatera Utara

Kalimantan Timur

Kalimantan Barat

Riau

Kalimantan Tengah

Sumatera Barat

Jambi

Kalimantan Selatan

Bengkulu

Sumatera Selatan

Java Sea

Lampung

Jakarta Raya

★ Jakarta

Jawa Barat

Jawa Tengah

Jawa Timur

Nusa Tenggara

Indian Ocean

Yogyakarta

Bali

Look at this map of Indonesia. Make a list of the oceans and seas that you notice. How many of each are there? What other waterways can you identify?

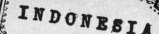

INDONESIA

PHILIPPINES

Sulu
Sea

*Celebes
Sea*

Sulawesi Utara

*Molucca
Sea*

*Pacific
Ocean*

awesi Tengah
si

Maluku

Sulawesi
Tenggara

INDONESIA

Irian Jaya

PAPUA
NEW
GUINEA

*Banda
Sea* Maluku

EAST TIMOR

Nusa Tenggara Timur

*Timor
Sea*

*Arafura
Sea*

AUSTRALIA

For more Indonesian wonders, turn to the country's unique animal life. The babi rusa, a small pig, can only be found here. There are also animals that look like tiny deer. They stand less than 2 feet (0.6 m) tall. Many species of birds and insects flutter overhead. One of the most interesting animals is the Komodo dragon. It is the country's national animal. It can grow to be 10 feet (3.0 m) long and weigh more than 300 pounds (136.1 kg). The creature is extremely fast. With its sharp claws, notched teeth, and powerful jaws, it is easy to understand why it reminds many people of a dinosaur.

◆ Komodo dragons are dangerous animals, but they rarely attack humans.

CHAPTER TWO

BUSINESS AND GOVERNMENT IN INDONESIA

↜ Rice is both an important cash crop and a large part of Indonesian meals.

What kinds of jobs can you imagine people who live on islands doing? In the past, many people were farmers. Over time, this number has dropped. The country's biggest crop is rice. It is grown in huge fields called **paddies**.

Fishing is one common occupation in Indonesia. Some people catch just enough to feed their families. Others supply companies with enough fish to ship to other parts of the world.

Indonesian money is called rupiah (roo-PEE-uh). Bills come in many amounts, including 100, 10,000, and 100,000 rupiah. In 2010, one U.S. dollar equaled approximately 9,091 rupiah.

◆ Oil drilling facilities can be spotted throughout the waters surrounding Indonesia's many islands.

Oil production is a very important part of Indonesia's economy. Every year, it **exports** billions of dollars worth of oil, natural gas, and coal. These products are sent to places such as Japan, the United States, and China. Some of the country's most valuable resources can be found underground. The soil is rich in materials such as nickel, tin, silver, and uranium.

It is estimated that about 42 percent of Indonesian people work in agriculture. Nearly 19 percent work in industrial jobs such as factory work, mining, or construction. Slightly more than 39 percent hold service jobs. Some examples of service workers are teachers, waiters, and police officers..

Create a pie chart that shows these 3 parts of Indonesia's labor force. Use a piece of paper to trace the blank pie chart shown here. Decide which sections represent agricultural workers, industrial workers, and service workers. Label each section. Then color each part of the pie a different color. Which part of the pie is the biggest? Which is the smallest?

STOP Don't write in this book!

The type of work Indonesians do often depends on what island they live on and what is and is not available there. Those closest to the ocean often fish. People in large cities might work in hotels or restaurants. People living on islands with the largest rice paddies might be farmers. Some Indonesians are experts with wood. They might make a living carving statues and spirit poles. Many women in Indonesia specialize in making a cloth called batik. This involves painting, applying wax, and dying cloth to create fabric with intricate patterns. Women who live near **fertile** riverbeds often make beautiful handmade pottery. Those near forests or bamboo groves focus on making baskets, mats, and hats from the plants.

➥ Batik is known for its beautiful handmade patterns.

Have you ever seen a picture of a rickshaw? In Indonesia, these three-wheeled cycles are called becaks. They used to be one of the main ways people traveled in the bigger cities. They were banned from the big cities because they caused major traffic jams. Despite the ban, you can still catch a ride in one in the smaller cities. Each one is unique because owners often decorate them with beads and colorful scarves.

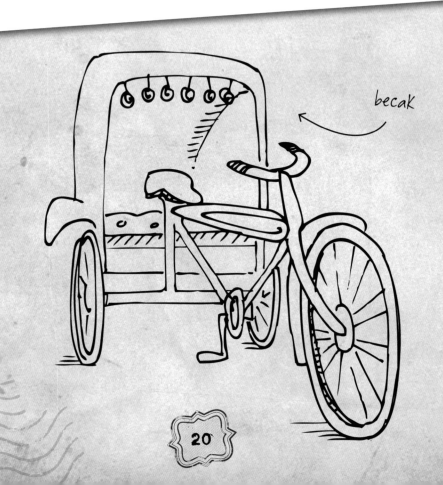

becak

◆◆ Working in a rice paddy is one job often done by those with little or no education.

Indonesians are very hard workers. Even so, many struggle to make enough money. Approximately 40 million Indonesians live below the poverty line. If someone lives below the poverty line, he does not make enough money to meet basic needs such as food and housing. Some people—including children—take to the streets as beggars. Many people who struggle to make a living have little or no education. In some places, there aren't enough teachers to lead classes. Schooling is expensive, too. Many parents cannot afford to educate their children. Some children end up helping their families grow crops, run businesses, or take care of their homes. Only the wealthy can afford to send their children to private schools.

IMPORT EXPORT

Do you want to know more about Indonesia's economy? Take a look at its trading partners. Trading partners are the countries that **import** goods from a country or export goods to that country. Here is a graph showing the countries that are India's top import and export trading partners.

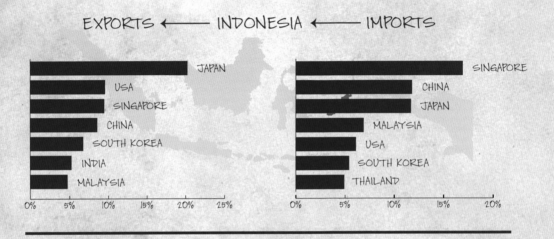

EXPORTS ← INDONESIA ← IMPORTS

EXPORTS
- JAPAN
- USA
- SINGAPORE
- CHINA
- SOUTH KOREA
- INDIA
- MALAYSIA

0% 5% 10% 15% 20% 25%

IMPORTS
- SINGAPORE
- CHINA
- JAPAN
- MALAYSIA
- USA
- SOUTH KOREA
- THAILAND

0% 5% 10% 15% 20%

As in the United States, Indonesia has a government with three branches: executive, legislative, and judicial. The president acts as both the head of the government and the chief of state. He or she is the head of the executive branch. The legislative branch is under the control of the 700-member People's Consultative Assembly. The judicial branch is headed by the Supreme Court. Its judges are appointed by the president.

Susilo Bambang Yudhoyono became president of Indonesia in 2004. SBY, as he is known, was re-elected in 2009. Indonesians have been able to directly elect their president since 2004. Before that, Indonesia experienced a 32-year period of military rule, which ended in 1998.

Susilo Bambang Yudhoyono

It is a challenge to fairly and efficiently govern a country that is made up of thousands of islands. The people of Indonesia come from more than 300 ethnic groups. They speak almost 400 different languages. Let's find out more about Indonesia's people!

The Indonesian flag was adopted in 1945. It has a red stripe on top and a white one on the bottom. The red stands for courage and freedom. The white is for justice and purity.

A PEOPLE SEPARATED

↔ Indonesia is home to a wide range of cultures.

Indonesia's motto is "Unity through **Diversity**."
Remaining united when separated by so many miles of
land and ocean is not easy. There are many differences
in language, customs, and religious beliefs.

No matter what island Indonesians live on, family is very important. Babies are cherished. They are kept close in a loved one's arms or in slings for the first 2 years of their lives. Children are considered family treasures.

With more than 300 ethnic groups spread out across the islands, there are many different kinds of lifestyles. The people of Java are called Javanese. They are the

◆ In Indonesia, it is common for several generations of a family to share a home.

➥ Every Indonesian cultural group has its own ways of dressing, communicating, and celebrating.

largest ethnic group. Nearly all Indonesians speak a common language known as Bahasa Indonesia. In addition, groups such as the Javanese have their own way of speaking. They use three different levels of speech: formal, semiformal, and informal. How words are spoken reveals a person's status and age. It also reflects how well people know the others they are talking to. The Sudanese also live on Java. They are the second largest ethnic group. They have three levels of speech, too. They are called refined, medium, and vulgar.

How many ways can you think of to say no? Take out a piece of paper and list them. Include all of the phrases you can come up with. "No, thank you" is one example. The Indonesians have many words or phrases that imply "no." Each one has a slightly different meaning. Look at this list! Try thinking of situations in which these terms might be used.

belum	(not yet)
jangan	(don't!)
terima kasih	(no, thank you)

The word tidak is also used in a variety of ways.
Here are some examples:

tidak usah	(not necessary)
lebih baik tidak	(not a good idea)
tidak boleh	(not allowed to)
tidak senang	(not happy)
tidak terima	(don't approve)
maaf tidak	(no, sorry)

Some of Indonesia's ethnic groups have not changed in many years. The Badui live in the remote parts of Java. Many of them believe they are directly descended from the gods. The Minangkabau people of Sumatra follow a lifestyle in which the women are in charge. Everything of value is passed from mother to daughter. On Bali, the Balinese have set up villages that center on different professions. If you are a painter, for example, you would likely live in Ubud. If you are skilled at carving wood, you would live in Mas.

➦ Many Indonesians live exactly as their ancestors have for hundreds of years.

■► Indonesia's leaders are working to bring better education to the country's children.

Many Indonesian children go to elementary school. Less than half, however, continue their education after the age of 12. Less than half of those who go on to high school graduate. To help improve this problem, the government has been expanding its education budget and setting new goals.

Nearly 90 percent of Indonesians are Muslim. They follow the teachings of Islam. On some islands, however, other religions are practiced. These include Hinduism, Buddhism, and Christianity. On some of the most remote islands, **animism**, or the belief in spirits, ghosts, and genies, is common. Animism also involves the belief that spirits live within natural things such as rocks and trees. **Atheism** is not allowed.

Most Muslims follow the Five Pillars of Islam. They include:
- Declaring their belief that God is the only god and that Muhammad is the messenger of God
- Praying five times each day
- Donating money to charity
- Fasting and self-purification during certain times
- Making a journey to Mecca at least once in a person's lifetime

Mecca

Just as languages and customs change from island to island, so does music. Gamelan music is performed on drums, gongs, and xylophones. It can be heard throughout Indonesia. Young people like to listen to dangdut. It's a combination of Western-style rock and Arab pop music. Kroncong is another style that combines elements of European and Indonesian music.

☛ Gamelan orchestras often perform at celebrations such as weddings and festivals.

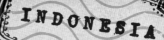

CHAPTER FOUR

TIME FOR FUN!

●◦ Dancers in colorful costumes can be seen at many Indonesian celebrations.

Whether they are celebrating the end of Ramadan or welcoming the arrival of a new year, Indonesians like to have fun. Festivals often involve music, singing, dancing, parties, and parades.

In the past, warriors had to be able to jump over any obstacle in their way. Today, that tradition continues on Nias Island, 75 miles (120.7 km) west of Sumatra. Young men take part in stone jumping competitions. They run and jump over a 5-foot (1.5 m) high, 1.5-foot (0.5 m) wide stone wall—some of them with sword in hand.

Sports are important to many Indonesians. One favorite game is **badminton**. The country is known internationally for the skill of its players. Every 4 years, the country hosts the *Pekan Olahraga Nasional*. It's a multisport competition held in different parts of Indonesia that lasts for several days.

Have you ever been to a puppet show? In Indonesia, they have many of them. They are not necessarily for children. Shadow puppetry shows, or *wayang kulit*, typically tell stories about the country's history and honor its heroes. They are performed with flat puppets that are painted colorfully and feature many details. Shows often run all night.

Indonesian music often features many different instruments, including cymbals. Here is a great way to make your own mini cymbals for the next time you celebrate an occasion.

MATERIALS

- 2 metal food jar lids (the lids of baby food jars work well)
- elastic that is 0.25 to 0.5 inches (0.6 to 1.3 centimeters) wide
- scissors
- hammer
- nail
- paints
- paintbrush
- glue
- sequins, beads, and stickers

INSTRUCTIONS

1. Cut two 4-inch (10.2 cm) pieces of elastic.
2. Ask an adult to a punch a hole in the center of each jar lid using the hammer and nail. Be careful not to damage the work surface with the nail. Set the hammer and nail aside once the holes are created.

3. Take one length of elastic and work both ends through the hole of one lid. You are creating a loop for your finger.

4. Tie the ends of the elastic into a knot on the opposite side of the lid.

5. Repeat Step #3 and Step #4 with the second length of elastic and lid.

6. Next comes the fun part: decorating! Get creative and use paints, sequins, stickers, or whatever else you like to decorate your cymbals.

7. Allow any paint or glue to dry completely.

Ready to make music? Slip your thumb into the elastic loop of one cymbal. Slip the pointer or middle finger of the same hand into the loop of the second cymbal. Work your fingers to make the cymbals clank together.

Independence Day is an important time in Indonesia. It is a holiday for all Indonesians, regardless of what island they live on, what religion they follow, or what language they speak. High-rise office buildings feature banners or lighted displays. The fences around government offices are decorated with red and white fabric. Stores hold special sales and everyone displays the words, *Dirgahayu RI* or "Long Live Indonesia." When the day finally arrives, the flag is raised and parades are held. Happy Independence Day, Indonesia!

❖ Indonesian Independence Day parades often feature members of the military or war veterans.

These are some of the holidays that are celebrated in Indonesia:

January 1	New Year's Day
January	Idul Adha (return of pilgrims from Mecca)
January or February	Imlek (Chinese New Year)
January or February	Muharram (Islamic New Year)
March	Hari Raya Nyepi Tahun Baru (Hindu New Year)
March or April	Easter
March or April	Nyepi (Balinese New Year)
April or May	Maulud Nabi Muhammad (birthday of the Prophet)
May	Waisak Day (Buddha Day)
August 17	Hari Proklamasi Kemerdekaan/ Independence Day
August or September	Isra Miraj Nabi Muhammad (ascension of the Prophet)
September or October	Idul Fitri or Lebaran (end of Ramadan)
December	Islamic New Year
December 25	Christmas Day

CHAPTER FIVE

DINNERTIME

➥ Seafood, such as shrimp, is found in many Indonesian dishes.

Can you imagine what food is like in Indonesia? Thanks to its fertile soil and warm climate, there is always a lot of fresh produce to choose from. The oceans provide many kinds of seafood.

Fruit is common in Indonesian meals and there are many choices. Coconut milk, oil, and meat are all used to flavor foods. Vegetables include the leaves of bamboo and **cassava** plants.

durian

It looks like a spiky football. When it is cut open, it smells like a combination of stinky socks and rotten eggs. It is a durian—called "The King of Fruits" in Indonesia and other Asian countries. If you can get past the smell and manage to take a bite, you may be surprised at how tasty it is! The center is creamy and tastes a lot like vanilla pudding. It is used in many dishes throughout Indonesia.

→ If you visit Indonesia, you might eat rice at every meal of the day.

The recipes found throughout Indonesia depend largely on which ethnic groups live in the region. In Sumatra, you might have an Indian dish with lots of curry. Some Indonesian dishes are influenced by Chinese cooking. A few examples include Chinese noodles and meatballs. No matter where you go, however, you are likely to have rice. It is the most commonly eaten food throughout the country. It is used in dishes for breakfast, lunch, dinner, and even dessert.

One of the best ways to learn about another country is to sample its foods. Try making this easy snack called acar, or pickles. Be sure to have an adult help with any chopping.

Acar

INGREDIENTS

1 cup of cucumbers, sliced thick

1 carrot, sliced thin

1 small green onion, sliced

2 tablespoons (29.6 milliliters) of sugar

½ teaspoon (2.5 ml) of salt

1 tablespoon (14.8 ml) of distilled white vinegar

1 tablespoon (14.8 ml) of water

3 to 5 hot green or red chili peppers (optional)

Instructions are on the following page →

INSTRUCTIONS

1. Combine all of the ingredients together in a bowl. If you like spicy foods, add the chilies to the mix.
2. Mix well using salad tongs.
3. Let the mixture sit for 2 hours.

Serve at room temperature.

↝ Try eating your acar with some rice!

❖ Coconuts and their milk can be used to create a wide variety of delicious dishes.

Sauces add spice and flavor to many Indonesian recipes. Coconut milk is often poured over dishes. It helps balance the heat of the peppers that are found in many recipes. Another favorite is *kecap manis*, a sweet soy sauce. It is made from soybeans, sugar, anise, and other ingredients.

Indonesia has its share of struggles. But it is also a land of striking landscapes and interesting cultures. Which island will you visit first?

GLOSSARY

animism (AN-ih-miz-uhm) the belief that natural objects possess souls

archipelago (ar-kuh-PEH-luh-goh) a large group or chain of islands

atheism (AY-thee-iz-uhm) the belief that there is no God

badminton (BAD-min-tuhn) a game played on a court with two or four players with rackets and an object called a shuttlecock

cassava (kuh-SAH-vuh) a starch-producing plant

corpse (KORPS) a dead body

diversity (di-VUR-sih-tee) variety or difference

exports (EK-sportss) act of selling something to another country or products sold in this way

fertile (FUR-tuhl) capable of bearing or producing vegetation or offspring

import (IM-port) bring in from another country

paddies (PAD-eez) wet rice fields

tsunami (tsoo-NAH-mee) a large wave caused by underwater volcanoes or earthquakes

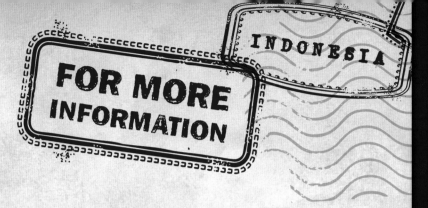

FOR MORE INFORMATION

Books

Gerner, Katy. *Islam*. New York: Marshall Cavendish Benchmark, 2008.

Lim, Robin. *Indonesia*. Minneapolis: Lerner Publishing Group, 2010.

Ryan, Patrick. *Welcome to Indonesia*. Mankato, MN: Child's World, 2008.

Web Sites

BBC—Key Musical Features: Gamelan
www.bbc.co.uk/schools/gcsebitesize/music/worldmusic/indiatoindonesiarev5.shtml
Find out more about Gamelan music.

Central Intelligence Agency—The World Factbook: Indonesia
www.cia.gov/library/publications/the-world-factbook/geos/id.html
Check out this site for information about Indonesia's economy, geography, population, and government.

National Geographic Kids—Komodo Dragons
kids.nationalgeographic.com/Animals/CreatureFeature/Komodo-dragon
Learn more about one of Indonesia's most interesting creatures.

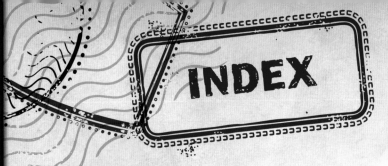

INDEX

ABOUT THE AUTHOR
Tamra Orr is the author of more than 200 books for readers of all ages. Her favorite part of writing books is learning fascinating new things about the world and its people. She and her family live in the Pacific Northwest.